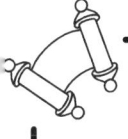

I Spy Hanukkah:

With Coloring Pages

This Book Belongs To:

_____

Hanukkah Sameach!

Coperything By Joshua Tigger Publishing

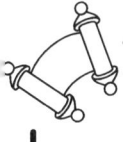

TEST COLOR PAGE

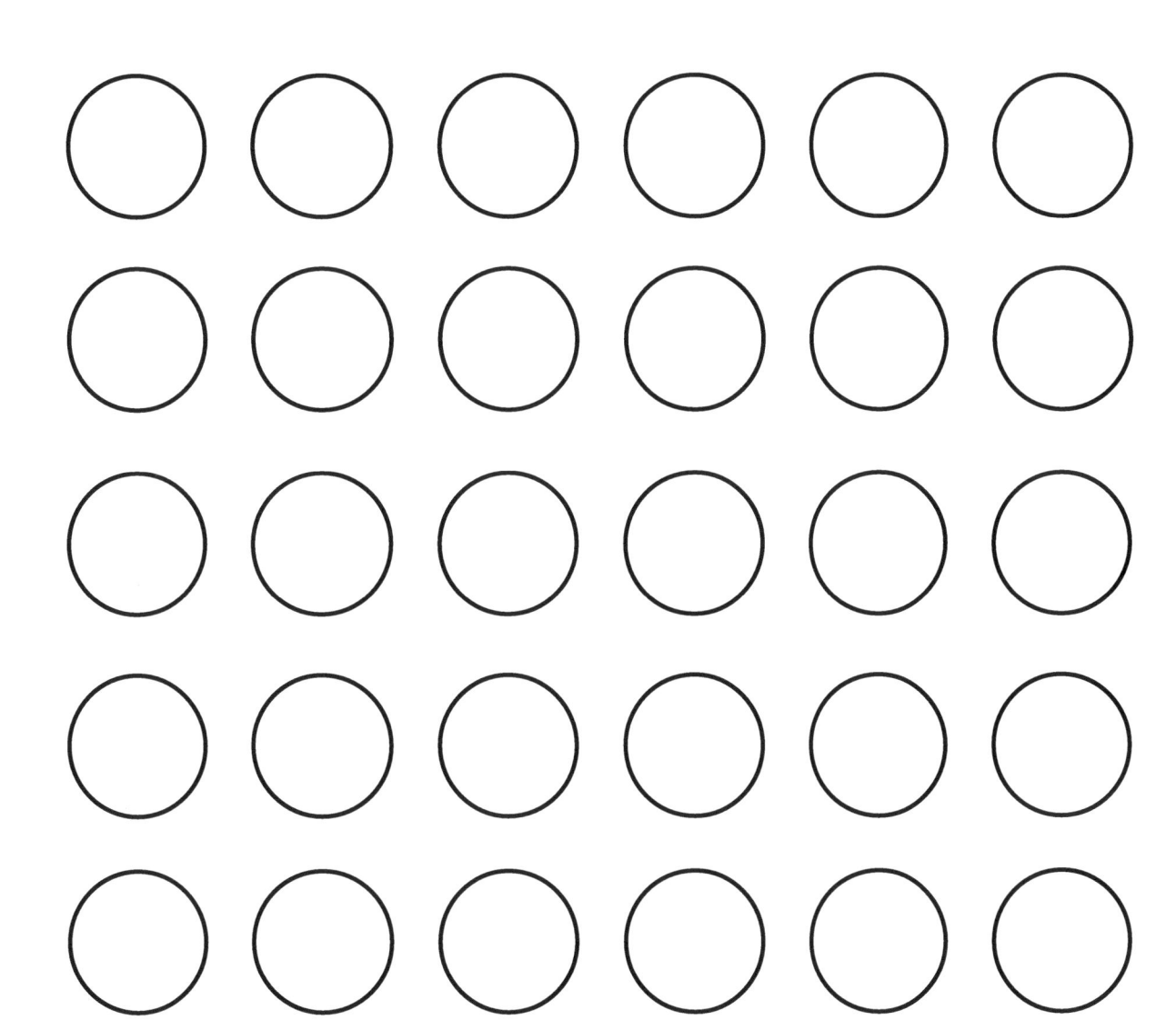

SINGLE-SIDED PAGES - EVERY IMAGE IS PLACED ON ITS OWN PAGE TO REDUCE THE BLEED-THROUGH PROBLEM FOUND IN OTHER COLORING BOOKS

JOSHUA TIGGER PUBLISHING

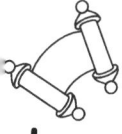

I Spy with my little eye something starting with:

L

SINGLE-SIDED PAGES - EVERY IMAGE IS PLACED ON ITS OWN PAGE TO REDUCE THE BLEED-THROUGH PROBLEM FOUND IN OTHER COLORING BOOKS

JOSHUA TIGGER PUBLISHING

L is for

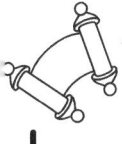

LATKES

SINGLE-SIDED PAGES - EVERY IMAGE IS PLACED ON ITS OWN PAGE TO REDUCE THE BLEED-THROUGH PROBLEM FOUND IN OTHER COLORING BOOKS

JOSHUA TIGGER PUBLISHING

I Spy with my little eye something starting with:

M

SINGLE-SIDED PAGES - EVERY IMAGE IS PLACED ON ITS OWN PAGE TO REDUCE THE BLEED-THROUGH PROBLEM FOUND IN OTHER COLORING BOOKS

JOSHUA TIGGER PUBLISHING

M is for

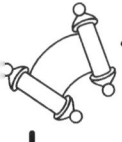

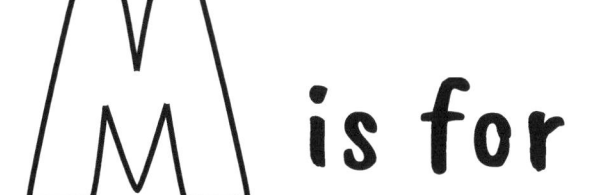

MENORAH

SINGLE-SIDED PAGES - EVERY IMAGE IS PLACED ON ITS OWN PAGE TO REDUCE THE BLEED-THROUGH PROBLEM FOUND IN OTHER COLORING BOOKS

JOSHUA TIGGER PUBLISHING

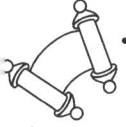

I Spy with my little eye something starting with:

SINGLE-SIDED PAGES - EVERY IMAGE IS PLACED ON ITS OWN PAGE TO REDUCE THE BLEED-THROUGH PROBLEM FOUND IN OTHER COLORING BOOKS

JOSHUA TIGGER PUBLISHING

C is for

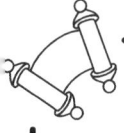

CHOCOLATE COINS

SINGLE-SIDED PAGES - EVERY IMAGE IS PLACED ON ITS OWN
PAGE TO REDUCE THE BLEED-THROUGH PROBLEM FOUND IN
OTHER COLORING BOOKS

JOSHUA TIGGER PUBLISHING

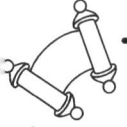

I Spy with my little eye something starting with:

D

SINGLE-SIDED PAGES - EVERY IMAGE IS PLACED ON ITS OWN PAGE TO REDUCE THE BLEED-THROUGH PROBLEM FOUND IN OTHER COLORING BOOKS

JOSHUA TIGGER PUBLISHING

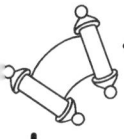

D is for

DOUGHNUTS

SINGLE-SIDED PAGES - EVERY IMAGE IS PLACED ON ITS OWN
PAGE TO REDUCE THE BLEED-THROUGH PROBLEM FOUND IN
OTHER COLORING BOOKS

JOSHUA TIGGER PUBLISHING

I Spy with my little eye something starting with:

G

SINGLE-SIDED PAGES - EVERY IMAGE IS PLACED ON ITS OWN PAGE TO REDUCE THE BLEED-THROUGH PROBLEM FOUND IN OTHER COLORING BOOKS

JOSHUA TIGGER PUBLISHING

G is for

GIFTS

SINGLE-SIDED PAGES - EVERY IMAGE IS PLACED ON ITS OWN PAGE TO REDUCE THE BLEED-THROUGH PROBLEM FOUND IN OTHER COLORING BOOKS

JOSHUA TIGGER PUBLISHING

I Spy with my little eye something starting with:

R

SINGLE-SIDED PAGES - EVERY IMAGE IS PLACED ON ITS OWN PAGE TO REDUCE THE BLEED-THROUGH PROBLEM FOUND IN OTHER COLORING BOOKS

JOSHUA TIGGER PUBLISHING

R is for

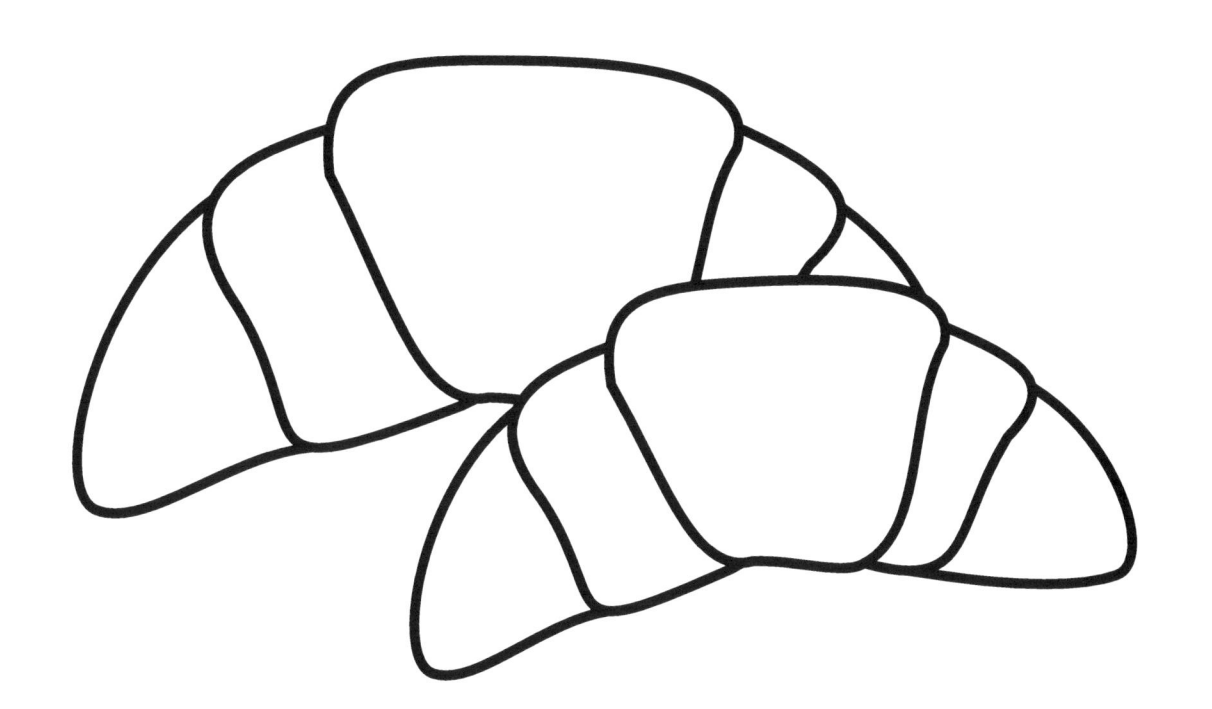

RUGELACH

SINGLE-SIDED PAGES - EVERY IMAGE IS PLACED ON ITS OWN PAGE TO REDUCE THE BLEED-THROUGH PROBLEM FOUND IN OTHER COLORING BOOKS

JOSHUA TIGGER PUBLISHING

I Spy with my little eye something starting with:

D

SINGLE-SIDED PAGES - EVERY IMAGE IS PLACED ON ITS OWN
PAGE TO REDUCE THE BLEED-THROUGH PROBLEM FOUND IN
OTHER COLORING BOOKS

JOSHUA TIGGER PUBLISHING

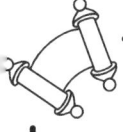

D is for
DREIDELS

SINGLE-SIDED PAGES - EVERY IMAGE IS PLACED ON ITS OWN
PAGE TO REDUCE THE BLEED-THROUGH PROBLEM FOUND IN
OTHER COLORING BOOKS

JOSHUA TIGGER PUBLISHING

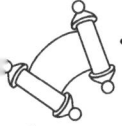

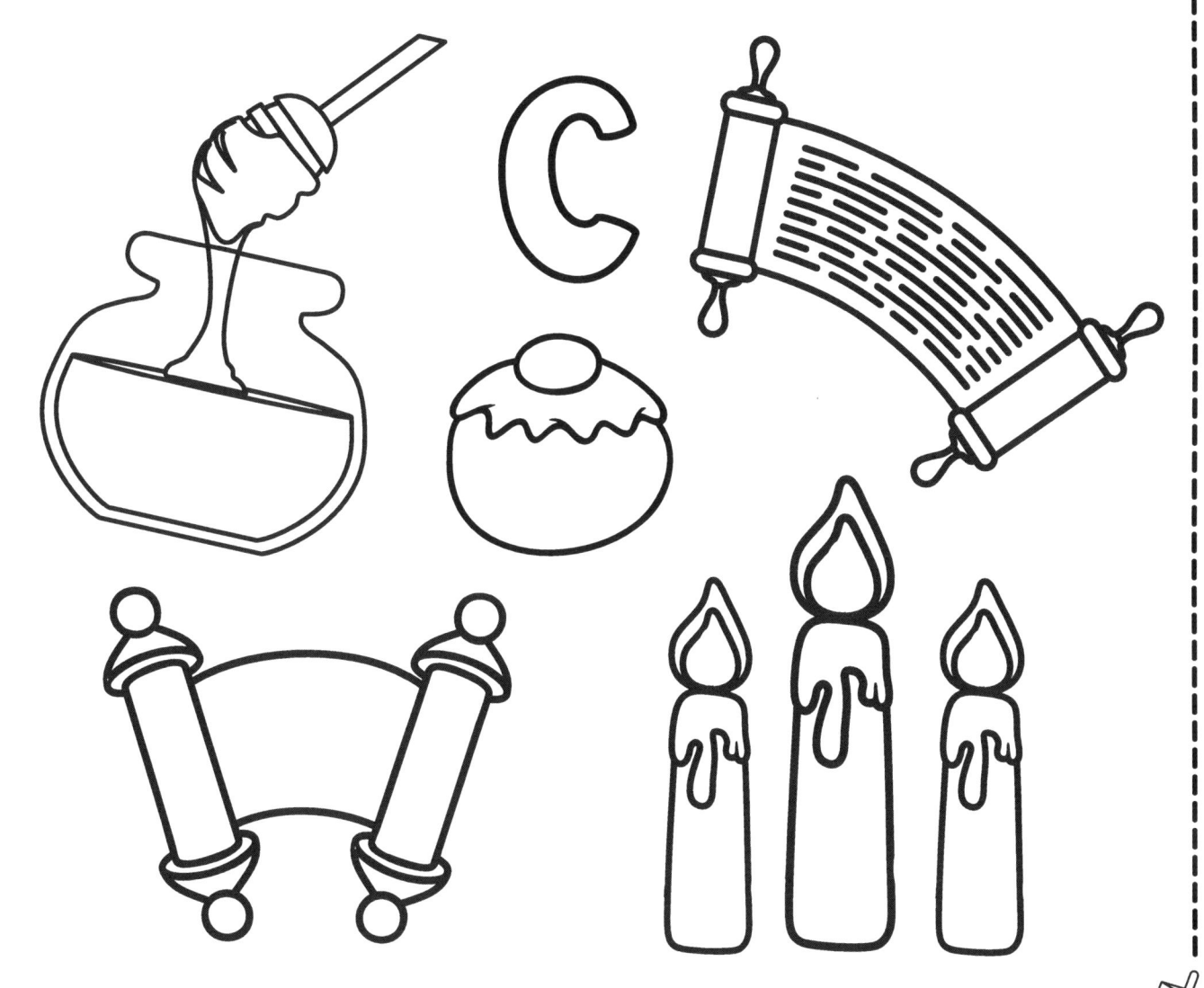

I Spy with my little eye something starting with:

SINGLE-SIDED PAGES - EVERY IMAGE IS PLACED ON ITS OWN
PAGE TO REDUCE THE BLEED-THROUGH PROBLEM FOUND IN
OTHER COLORING BOOKS

JOSHUA TIGGER PUBLISHING

C is for CANDLES

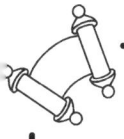

SINGLE-SIDED PAGES - EVERY IMAGE IS PLACED ON ITS OWN PAGE TO REDUCE THE BLEED-THROUGH PROBLEM FOUND IN OTHER COLORING BOOKS

JOSHUA TIGGER PUBLISHING

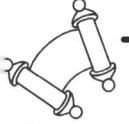

I Spy with my little eye something starting with:

SINGLE-SIDED PAGES - EVERY IMAGE IS PLACED ON ITS OWN
PAGE TO REDUCE THE BLEED-THROUGH PROBLEM FOUND IN
OTHER COLORING BOOKS

JOSHUA TIGGER PUBLISHING

T is for

TORAH

SINGLE-SIDED PAGES - EVERY IMAGE IS PLACED ON ITS OWN PAGE TO REDUCE THE BLEED-THROUGH PROBLEM FOUND IN OTHER COLORING BOOKS

JOSHUA TIGGER PUBLISHING

I Spy with my little eye something starting with:

S

SINGLE-SIDED PAGES - EVERY IMAGE IS PLACED ON ITS OWN PAGE TO REDUCE THE BLEED-THROUGH PROBLEM FOUND IN OTHER COLORING BOOKS

JOSHUA TIGGER PUBLISHING

S is for

STAR

SINGLE-SIDED PAGES - EVERY IMAGE IS PLACED ON ITS OWN PAGE TO REDUCE THE BLEED-THROUGH PROBLEM FOUND IN OTHER COLORING BOOKS

JOSHUA TIGGER PUBLISHING

I Spy with my little eye something starting with:

H

SINGLE-SIDED PAGES - EVERY IMAGE IS PLACED ON ITS OWN PAGE TO REDUCE THE BLEED-THROUGH PROBLEM FOUND IN OTHER COLORING BOOKS

JOSHUA TIGGER PUBLISHING

H is for

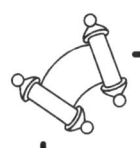

HONEY

SINGLE-SIDED PAGES - EVERY IMAGE IS PLACED ON ITS OWN PAGE TO REDUCE THE BLEED-THROUGH PROBLEM FOUND IN OTHER COLORING BOOKS

JOSHUA TIGGER PUBLISHING

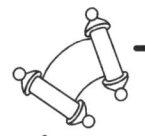

I Spy with my little eye something starting with:

W

SINGLE-SIDED PAGES - EVERY IMAGE IS PLACED ON ITS OWN
PAGE TO REDUCE THE BLEED-THROUGH PROBLEM FOUND IN
OTHER COLORING BOOKS

JOSHUA TIGGER PUBLISHING

W is for
WINE

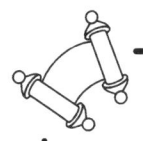

SINGLE-SIDED PAGES - EVERY IMAGE IS PLACED ON ITS OWN PAGE TO REDUCE THE BLEED-THROUGH PROBLEM FOUND IN OTHER COLORING BOOKS

JOSHUA TIGGER PUBLISHING

I Spy with my little eye something starting with:

SINGLE-SIDED PAGES - EVERY IMAGE IS PLACED ON ITS OWN
PAGE TO REDUCE THE BLEED-THROUGH PROBLEM FOUND IN
OTHER COLORING BOOKS

JOSHUA TIGGER PUBLISHING

C is for

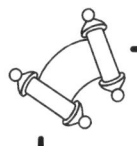

CHALLAH

SINGLE-SIDED PAGES - EVERY IMAGE IS PLACED ON ITS OWN PAGE TO REDUCE THE BLEED-THROUGH PROBLEM FOUND IN OTHER COLORING BOOKS

JOSHUA TIGGER PUBLISHING

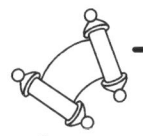

I Spy with my little eye something starting with:

P

SINGLE-SIDED PAGES - EVERY IMAGE IS PLACED ON ITS OWN PAGE TO REDUCE THE BLEED-THROUGH PROBLEM FOUND IN OTHER COLORING BOOKS

JOSHUA TIGGER PUBLISHING

P is for
PITCHER

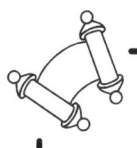

SINGLE-SIDED PAGES - EVERY IMAGE IS PLACED ON ITS OWN
PAGE TO REDUCE THE BLEED-THROUGH PROBLEM FOUND IN
OTHER COLORING BOOKS

JOSHUA TIGGER PUBLISHING

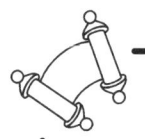

I Spy with my little eye something starting with:

SINGLE-SIDED PAGES - EVERY IMAGE IS PLACED ON ITS OWN PAGE TO REDUCE THE BLEED-THROUGH PROBLEM FOUND IN OTHER COLORING BOOKS

JOSHUA TIGGER PUBLISHING

C is for
CHALICE

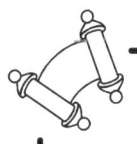

SINGLE-SIDED PAGES - EVERY IMAGE IS PLACED ON ITS OWN PAGE TO REDUCE THE BLEED-THROUGH PROBLEM FOUND IN OTHER COLORING BOOKS

JOSHUA TIGGER PUBLISHING

I Spy with my little eye something starting with:

K

SINGLE-SIDED PAGES - EVERY IMAGE IS PLACED ON ITS OWN PAGE TO REDUCE THE BLEED-THROUGH PROBLEM FOUND IN OTHER COLORING BOOKS

JOSHUA TIGGER PUBLISHING

K is for

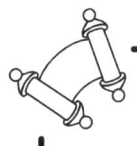

KIPPAH

SINGLE-SIDED PAGES - EVERY IMAGE IS PLACED ON ITS OWN PAGE TO REDUCE THE BLEED-THROUGH PROBLEM FOUND IN OTHER COLORING BOOKS

JOSHUA TIGGER PUBLISHING

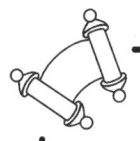

I Spy with my little eye something starting with:

C

SINGLE-SIDED PAGES - EVERY IMAGE IS PLACED ON ITS OWN PAGE TO REDUCE THE BLEED-THROUGH PROBLEM FOUND IN OTHER COLORING BOOKS

JOSHUA TIGGER PUBLISHING

C is for

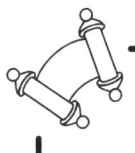

CANDIES

SINGLE-SIDED PAGES - EVERY IMAGE IS PLACED ON ITS OWN PAGE TO REDUCE THE BLEED-THROUGH PROBLEM FOUND IN OTHER COLORING BOOKS

JOSHUA TIGGER PUBLISHING

I AM VERY GRATEFUL FOR PURCHASING THIS BOOK. I HOPE YOU WILL SPEND AN UNFORGETTABLE TIME WITH YOUR CHILD, HAVING FUN AND LEARNING FROM THIS BOOK

IF IT WOULD NOT BE A PROBLEM FOR YOU I WOULD BE EXTREMELY GRATEFUL FOR LEAVING A REVIEW ON AMAZON. WE ARE A SMALL FAMILY BUSINESS AND THROUGH REVIEWS, WE CAN REACH MORE PEOPLE.

THANK YOU AGAIN FOR YOUR PURCHASE AND YOUR TRUST. I WISH YOU ENJOY YOUR BOOK AND HAVE A GREAT TIME WITH YOUR FAMILY

HANUKKAH SAMEACH!

WE HOPE THE BOOK HAS MET YOUR EXPECTATIONS, IF YOU FOUND ANY MISTAKES IN THE BOOK PLEASE CONTACT US BY EMAIL, AND WE WILL CORRECT THEM AS SOON AS POSSIBLE.

office.dannyd@gmail.com

INDEPENDENTLY PUBLISHED
Joshua Tigger Publishing

ILLUSTRATIONS:
FREEPIK

Manufactured by Amazon.ca
Bolton, ON